SMOKESCREENS

By J.T.C.

My deepest appreciation to Dr. Alberto Rivera for his help in awakening us to the dangers facing the believers in Christ.

Outside the U.S. call for a distributor nearest you or see our entire listing on the internet at: www. chick.com/distrib.asp

153/C

ISBN: 0-937958-14-X

Published by Chick Publications
P.O. Box 3500, Ontario, Calif. 91761-1019 USA
Tel: (909) 987-0771
Fax: (909) 941-8128
Internet: www.chick.com
E-Mail: postmaster@chick.com

Printed in the United States of America

Contents

INTRODUCTION

Greetings in the precious name of our Lord Jesus Christ. What you are going to read in this book is absolutely devastating. The information and the facts we're going to present are going to change your life. Be patient with me and please follow through to the end of the book. You'll never be the same.

Most of you know from studying your Bibles that Satan will build a false superchurch: the whore of Revelation, chapters 6, 13, 17 and 18. According to Bible prophecy, she will have great political, economic, military, and educational power, and she will persecute and murder the true believers in Christ.

I always used to wonder how Satan would be able to pull this off right under Christians' noses without them being aware of what was happening, and fighting back. But Satan is the master deceiver and I am beginning to see how he has cleverly set up smokescreens to hide the identity of the whore from the majority of Christian believers.

Let me explain what I mean by a smokescreen. In warfare, you have enemy action. When they're moving in, they set up a smokescreen. And the smoke confuses everyone so that you don't know where your enemies are. That's one technique. The other is a fifth column where you have a country that's about to fall. So you send in agents and they wear the people down saying it's hopeless, or saying, no, the enemy isn't really going to attack. And they, in a sense, put up their own smokescreens to confuse the issue before the assault comes.

I believe an assault is coming by the whore of Revelation. I believe they are setting up smokescreens, and that there are others within the Christian community that are setting up smokescreens. Now, we believe at Chick Publications, that the whore of Revelation is the Roman Catholic Institution. Our position is not something new. During the Reformation you had men like Martin Luther, John Knox, Calvin, a great number of them; and then the great preachers like Moody, Finney, Spurgeon and so on, they all believed the same thing, that the Vatican was the whore. It wasn't until lately that things have changed.

You see, the Jesuits influenced people and they started setting up smokescreens during our times, through our theological seminaries, and when that smokescreen came up we started seeing the whore of Revelation in a different light. They said, "Oh, no, this is something coming in the future." Or, "That happened 'way back in the past.'" This is done to confuse the Christians. Today, many people believe this. They have been beguiled like I was when I first listened to some of these people. It was a clever smokescreen. I was confused at first, but now I see the whore in her fullness, and it is scary.

I want to show you in this book some of her activities in the past, what she's doing today and what her ultimate goal is for the future. Some will be overwhelmed when they hear this message, but I believe with all my heart that this information must be told. People must be aware of what's going on and how Satan is working to destroy the work of God in these closing hours.

There has been a multi-million dollar campaign made through the media to convince people that I am a bigoted, anti-Catholic, hate literature publisher. And do you know something? They have been very effective in convincing people that this is what I am. The truth is, I love Catholic people enough to risk my life and my business to reach them with the gospel of Christ to pull them out of the false religious system they're now serving. I know what this system has done in the past and what it is planning for the future. I believe you'll understand when I've finished this message, where I'm coming from. But before we get started, let's go into prayer.

Dear heavenly Father and Lord, we come before you, and we thank you, Father, for Calvary, and your finished work, Lord, for the terrible price you paid for our sins so that we could be taken into the beloved. Father, we thank you that we can come before the throne of grace in boldness, and that you're a God who hears and answers prayer, Lord. That you protect and love, and watch over us. In Jesus' name we bind the forces of darkness surrounding anyone reading this book, and we loosen the angels of God to protect them against the attacks of satanic forces. I pray You will open their spiritual eyes and give them wisdom that they may understand. I bind any critical or self-righteous spirit in any of the readers, in Jesus' name. Lord, help us to be broken before you as we turn to you for our help. And Lord, we pray that as a result of this book, souls will be saved across this land, that a fire will start to burn in the hearts of Christians, that they will see who their enemy is, how Satan is moving and know how to combat it, Lord. In Jesus' name, we ask your help to win the victory over the powers of darkness. Open the eyes and ears of those who are reading, Father. Touch them and let them realize what's coming upon this earth. Let us be faithful, Lord, in your service. In Jesus' precious name, we pray. Amen.

CHAPTER ONE

THE WAFER-GOD

There are some Christians who are awake to what is going on, but there are many Christians today who believe everything is just fine. Everybody loves everybody else. The Christians, Mormons, Jews, Jehovah's Witnesses, Moslems are all serving the same God, but in different ways.

If I asked, "Can you partake of the Lord's Supper with Catholics?" They'd say, "Why not?" Let's find out if there is a difference between the Lord's Supper and the mass. Before I go on, let me explain that the bread, or wafer, used in the mass is called the host. When the host has been consecrated and offered as a sacrifice in the mass, it then becomes the eucharist. I am going to try to put into everyday language what is one of the great motivating forces behind the Roman Catholic Institution. It is the eucharist. I call it the little Jesus cookie. I know Catholics are going to be offended by this, but I can't help it. The Protestants have to realize where they stand on this thing.

CATHOLIC TWIN CIRCLE

The Roman Catholic Institution in their Canon laws state:

"If any one shall deny that the body and blood, together with the ***soul*** and ***divinity*** of our Lord Jesus Christ, and therefore entire Christ, are truly, really, and substantially contained in the sacrament of the most Holy Eucharist; and shall say that He is only in it as a sign, or in a figure, let him be accursed." (Accursed means to be damned, under a curse.)

"If any one shall say that Christ, the only begotten Son of God, is not to be adored ***in the holy sacrament of the Eucharist***,... and that He is not to be publicly set before the people to be adored, and that His adorers are idolaters, let him be accursed!"

John Paul II, IN THE SERVICE OF LOVE

That's when, beloved, the priest walks out holding up the cookie in the monstrance, which looks like a sunburst, and people come up and kiss it and adore it. And if any Protestant would say, "Hey, that's idolatry," that Protestant is to be accursed.

The Eucharist in the monstrance being carried in a procession.

Now, to sum this up, The Roman Catholic Institution teaches that you must believe that the bread, or host, consecrated in the mass actually becomes Jesus Christ and it is to be worshipped as

PERPETUAL ADORATION – Two Benedictine Sisters at the Convent of Perpetual Adoration kneel before the Blessed Sacrament exposed in a monstrance in the convent chapel. Whether at work or at prayer, the nuns focus their lives on Jesus present in the Eucharist.

God Almighty. This is why, back in 1554, a priest carrying the eucharist (the little Jesus cookie) could stand before a family of Christians in Scotland, tied to posts with dried brush up to their waists. He'd hold that piece of bread before them and ask if what he held in his hand was actually the body, blood and deity of Jesus Christ. When they said, "No, it is only a symbol," the priest's assistant placed his flaming torch into the brush and set those Bible-believers on fire. As the victims screamed in agony, the priest held up his crucifix and said, "All this is for the greater glory of God."

ALL THIS HISTORY HAS BEEN COVERED UP.

It holds firm, just as strong today, as it did in the time of the Middle Ages, that anyone who ridicules it, or says that it only represents Christ, is damned. The Vatican II Council re-affirmed this. Pope John XXIII said, "I do accept entirely all that has been decided and declared at the Council of Trent."

That Canon law is in effect today, beloved.

CHAPTER TWO

THE HAND OF ROME

This is a very difficult book to write. Many of you will think it is unbelievable. Yet, I believe we can prove our position historically and scripturally. Pay close attention to some of the quotes we are going to make. You will see how Satan is moving and closing in, in an attempt to destroy Bible Christianity.

I believe one of the reasons Protestants are so desperately weak today is the fact that history has been covered up. Books have been re-written. It only takes about two generations for everything to be forgotten, especially, if it is not told over and over again. It's like the holocaust of World War II. The Jews, thank God, are pressuring the networks to show films on the holocaust over and over on television, so that people will remember what happened. But you see, some things have been cleverly covered up and left to be forgotten. Most Christians know nothing of their heritage and the terrible price that was paid by those before us who stood against the Roman Catholic system.

Many of our young people have no concept of what an inquisition is. It is when a religious force moves in with such power, deception, and cruelty that it destroys everything standing in its way. Satan has dulled our hearing and thoughts concerning crimes of the past, and we as Americans cannot possibly conceive of such a thing happening here in our country. Is it possible?

The Christians of today are like little blades of grass, growing up in the sunshine, and there's a big lawn mower coming toward them – and it's singing hymns! It's the Roman Catholic

Institution. These are harsh words, but you must remember that the Roman Catholics believe with all their heart that their church is the church of Jesus Christ. They believe the pope is the vicar, or representative, of Jesus Christ on this earth. There is a teaching within the Roman Catholic structure called the temporal power. Temporal power means that the pope should control every person on the face of this globe, their property and their religion. The Jesuits are pushing for this temporal power which means a worldwide dictator. They believe this is the only way to go, and those who oppose them are the enemies of the gospel.

Here's something interesting. Trudeau, of Canada, who is surrounded by Jesuits, is setting up "civilian internment camps." That's just a fancy name for concentration camps. You can check this out in an article published in the Toronto Sun dated March 4, 1982. Now, that's just above our borders, beloved. I mentioned earlier that much of history has been covered up. Let's go back and look at the bloody history of the Vatican. Then you'll have the facts to decide for yourself whether or not she is the great whore. Let's go back in history now and touch on what took place in France at the St. Bartholomew massacre and what happened later in Ireland. We will then look at what took place in Yugoslavia during World War II.

On August 24, 1572, the bloody St. Bartholomew massacre began. This was to be one fatal blow to destroy the Protestant movement in France. The king of France had cleverly arranged a marriage between his sister and Henry of Navarre, head of the Protestant army. There was a great feast with much celebrating. After four days of feasting the soldiers were given a signal. At an hour before dawn, all the houses of the Protestants in the city were forced open at once. Admiral Coligny, the chief Protestant leader, was killed, his body thrown out of a window into the street where his head was cut off and sent to the pope. They also cut off his arms and privates and dragged him through the streets for three days until they finally hung his body by the heels outside the city.

The New Book of Martyrs

Massacre of Protestants on St. Bartholomew's Day

A scene from the Irish massacre in 1642 where 40,000 Protestants were inhumanly sacrificed by the Papists.

They also slaughtered many other well-know Protestants. In the first three days, over ten thousand were killed. The bodies were thrown into the river and blood ran through the streets into the river until it appeared like a stream of blood. So furious was their hellish rage that they even slew their own followers if they suspected that they were not very strong in their belief in the pope. From Paris, the destruction spread to all parts of the country. Over eight thousand more people were killed. Very few Protestants escaped the fury of their persecutors.

A similar massacre occurred in Ireland in 1641. The conspirators picked October 23, the feast of Ignatius Loyola, the founder of the Jesuit Order. They planned a general uprising for the whole country. All Protestants would be killed at once. To throw them off guard while the plan was being made, extra acts of kindness were shown to the Protestants. Early in the morning the conspirators were armed and every Protestant they could find was immediately murdered. They showed no mercy. From children to the aged, they were killed. Even invalids were not spared. They were caught by complete surprise. They had lived in peace and safety for years and now found no place to run. They were massacred by neighbors, friends, and even relatives.

Death often was the least they had to fear. Women were tied to posts, stripped to the waist, their breasts cut off with shears and left to bleed to death. Others who were pregnant were tied to tree branches, their unborn babies cut out and fed to the dogs while the husbands were forced to watch.

What you've just read is fully documented and historically factual. It is found in the Foxe's Book of Martyrs. Beloved, I want you to notice that both of these murderous assaults by the Vatican against the Christians in France and in Ireland followed a similar pattern. Before the attacks, there was a time of healing when the Roman Catholics became friendly and warm, and in both cases the Christians were so relieved that they let their guard down and assumed the Vatican had changed. **This** was their fatal mistake and it cost them their lives. I pray to God you will not forget what you've just read.

CHAPTER THREE

A 20th CENTURY INQUISITION

You may say, "Well, that was a long time ago. It's not like that anymore." But has the Vatican really changed? Let's look at her actions during World War II. Many of you have not

read our Crusaders book, **THE GODFATHERS,** or the book, **THE SECRET HISTORY OF THE JESUITS**, and, therefore, you don't really know what happened behind the scenes during World War II. So let me give you a brief picture of the conditions.

The Jesuits had secretly prepared World War II, and Hitler's war machine was built and financed by the Vatican to conquer the world for Roman Catholicism. Hitler, Mussolini, and Franco were to be the defenders of the faith. They were set up to win and conquer the world, and set up a millennium for the pope. Behind the scenes, the Jesuits controlled the Gestapo. All this is ***fully documented*** in **THE SECRET**

HISTORY OF THE JESUITS, published by Chick Publications.

Read what the press of the Spanish dictator, Franco, published on the 3rd of May 1945, the day of Hitler's death. It said, "Adolf Hitler, son of the Catholic Church, died while defending Christianity." It goes on to say, "Over his mortal remains stands his victorious moral figure. With the palm of the martyr, God gives Hitler the laurels of Victory."

Hitler himself stated, "I learned much from the Order of the Jesuits. Until now, there has never been anything more grandiose, on the earth, than the hierarchical organization of the Catholic church. I transferred much of this organization into my own party."

Walter Schellenberg, former chief of Nazi counter-espionage made this statement: "The S.S. organization had been constituted by Himmler according to the principles of the Jesuit Order. Their regulations and the Spiritual Exercises prescribed by Ignatius of Loyola were the model Himmler tried to copy exactly. Himmler's title as supreme chief of the S.S. was to be the equivalent of the Jesuits' 'General' and the whole structure was a close imitation of the Catholic Church's hierarchical order."

Franz von Papen, another powerful Nazi, who was instrumental in setting up the concordat between Germany and the Vatican had this to say: "The Third Reich is the first world power which not only acknowledges but also puts into practice the high principles of the papacy." If you are not aware of what a concordat is, a concordat is an agreement between the Vatican and a government. As far as the Vatican is concerned, that government that signed the concordat has now become a part of the government of God, and the Vatican fully intends to stabilize that government, give it divine protection, and give it international protection.

Like Italy, Germany signed a concordat with the Vatican in Rome, 1933.

Signing the concordat is Cardinal Pacelli (later to become Pope Pius XII). By 1933 he was the Vatican secretary of state. Second from the left is Franz Von Papen, a sinister Nazi and devout Roman Catholic who was Hitler's ace diplomat and the Vatican's agent in helping to bring Hitler to power.

Standing at the far right can be seen the little-known Vatican prelate, Montini, later to become Pope Paul VI.

The Godfathers, by Chick Publications, pg. 20.

Hitler with Reich Bishop Muller and Abbot Schachleiter, surrounded by party bosses; September 1934.

ADOLPH HITLER SAID:

"I am personally convinced of the great power and deep significance of Christianity, and I won't allow any other religion to be promoted. That is why I have turned away from Ludendorff and that is why I reject that book by Rosenberg. It was written by a Protestant. It is not a Party book. It was not written by him as a Party man. The Protestants can be left to argue with him… As a Catholic I never feel comfortable in the Evangelical Church or its structures. That is why I will have great difficulty if I try to regulate affairs of the Protestant churches. The evangelical people or the Protestants will in any case reject me. But you can be sure: I will protect the rights and freedoms of the churches and not let them be touched, so that you need have no fears about the future of the Church."

Hitler was also ready to discuss with the Bishop his views on the Jewish question: "As for the Jews, I am just carrying on with the same policy which the Catholic church has adopted for fifteen hundred years, when it has regarded the Jews as dangerous and pushed them into ghettos etc., because it knew what the Jews were like. I don't put race above religion, but I do see the danger in the representatives of this race for Church and State, and perhaps I am doing Christianity a great service."

Photo on opposite page and above quotes are from "The Nazi Persecution of the Churches" by J.S. Conway, Pgs. 25, 26, & 162

Bison Picture Library

Our Sunday Visitor, March 29,1981

The three big defenders of the Roman Catholic faith were Hitler, Mussolini, and Franco. All three had concordats with the Vatican. When the Nazi war machine swept through the Balkans on the way to attack Russia, Yugoslavia had become a Nazi occupied country.

The pope despised the Russian Orthodox members. They were called Serbians and they were marked for death in Yugoslavia. They were given one choice: to convert to Catholicism, or die.

Why were they killed? Why did the pope have such a vendetta against the Russian Orthodox? As we said in our Crusaders book, **The Godfathers**, the communist party was created by the Vatican to destroy one of her greatest enemies, The Russian Orthodox church. The communists had double-crossed the pope and refused to destroy the Russian Orthodox church members and at last, Pope Pius XII had created a machine to do what the communists had failed to do – butcher every Orthodox church member and their clergy. Let's see how this was accomplished.

Stane Kukavica, A Franciscan Monk, also seen in the uniform of the Ustashi.

The Catholic priests changed their robes for the uniforms of the dreaded Ustashi killer squads, and led the most barbaric, brutal raids upon those people and practiced satanic torture never before known in this century. We are not talking 800 years ago. We are talking 1940. I was in high school then.

The whore of Revelation showed her fangs, tore her enemies to shreds and cleverly covered up her crimes. All this is documented in many books, including **Catholic Terror Today**, by Avro Manhattan, the book the following quotes were taken from.

"The non-Catholic population of Catholic Croatia were given two basic alternatives: conversion or death. Their church buildings were closed, parish documents destroyed, ecclesiastical buildings burned down, Orthodox worshippers very often were arrested inside their own churches, and kept there or in local halls while awaiting their fate: forced conversion, concentration camps or execution. Their survival, more often than not, depended upon the whim of the Ustashi Commandants and of the Catholic Padres (priests) accompanying them."

Ante Pavelic, the head of the Ustashi state of Croatia, surrounded with Croatian Catholic clergy in April, 1942. He was to Yugoslavia, what Hitler was to Germany.

The bishops and archbishops of Croatia gave full support to the Ustashi. Here, the Croatian bishops and archbishops are seen pictured with Ante Pavelic during one of their frequent conferences with him.

Nuns marching together with Croatian Nazi-Legionnaires (Ustashi).

Pavelic among Croatian nuns. They were decorated (see decoration on chest) by Pavelic for their "Heroic" Ustashi deeds.

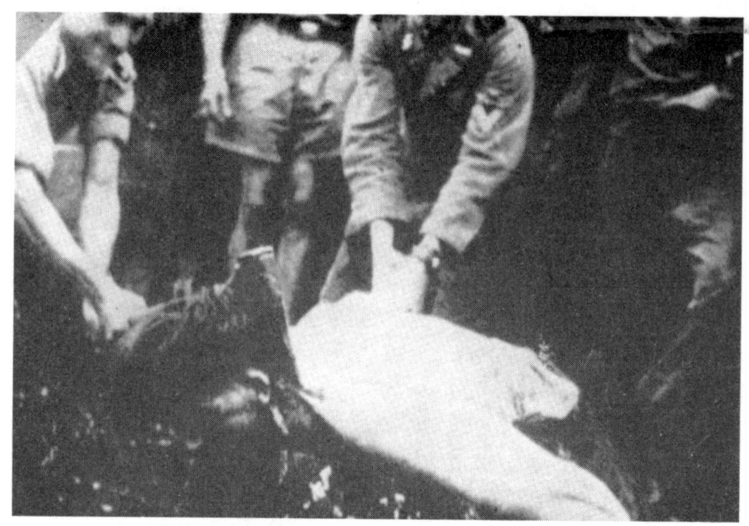

An Ustashi, with a sadistic smile on his face, chopping off a man's head with an ax.

This photograph of Ustashi taken in Bosnia in 1943 before they executed their victim.

"Mass murders were supplemented by the massacre of individuals, mostly in rural districts. The Ustashi very often used the most primitive weapons, such as forks, spades, hammers and saws, to torture their victims prior to their execution. They broke their legs, pulled off their skin and beards, blinded them by cutting their eyes with knives and even tearing them from their sockets." This information is documented by pictures and by the sworn testimony of survivors.

They did not spare women or children. To quote only one instance: 'In the villages between Vlasenica and Kladanj the Nazi occupational troops discovered children who had been impaled upon stakes by the Ustashi, their little members distorted with pain.' Catholic priests advocated the killing of children.

A priest named Ivan Raguz,repeatedly urged the killing of all Serbs, including children so that "not even the seeds of the beasts are left."

A Catholic priest named Juric said, "Today it is no longer a sin to kill a child of seven, should such a child be opposed to our movement of the Ustashi."

"The worst atrocities, strange as it may seem, were carried out by members of the intelligentsia. The case of Peter Brzica is undoubtedly one of the most incredible in this category. Peter Brzica had attended the Franciscan College at Siroki, Brijeg, in Herzegovina, was a law student, and a member of the Catholic organization of Crusaders. In the concentration camp at Jasenovac, on the night of August 29, 1942, orders were issued for executions. Bets were made as to who could liquidate the largest number of inmates. Peter Brzica cut the throats of 1,360 prisoners with a specially sharp butcher's knife. Having been proclaimed the prize-winner of the competition, he was elected King of the Cut-throats. A gold watch, a silver service and a roasted suckling pig and wine were his rewards."

The Franciscan monk, Miroslav Filipovic, left, as a priest, wearing his cassock, right, in Ustashi uniform. Filipovic was the commandant of the concentration camp at Jasenovac.

Jasenovac concentration camp distinguished itself because of the number of young inmates sent there. In 1942 the camp held over 24,000 Orthodox youngsters. Twelve thousand of them were murdered in cold blood.

Corpses of children starved to death in the concentration camp at Jasenovac.

Ustashi carrying the head of a Serbian Orthodox priest.

At Dubrovinick, Dalmatia, fascist soldiers had photographs of an Ustashi wearing two necklaces. One was a string of cut-out eyes, the other of torn out tongues of murdered Orthodox Serbs.

The atrocities of the Ustashi far surpassed mere physical torture. Their victims were tormented emotionally as well. An example of the unprecedented brutality is recorded by the sworn testimony of several witnesses regarding the following incident.

At Nevesinje, the Ustashi arrested one whole Serbian family consisting of father, mother and four children. The mother and children were separated from the father. For seven days they were tortured by starvation and thirst. Then they brought the mother and children a good-sized roast, and plenty of water to drink. These unfortunates were so hungry that they ate the entire roast. After they finished, The Ustashi told them that they had eaten the flesh of their father.

This happened in our generation, beloved. This is an example of the unleashed rage of the Vatican. I once read that, "Rome when in minority is as gentle as a lamb, when in equality is as clever as a fox, and when in majority is as fierce as a tiger." I believe that this is an accurate description.

CHAPTER FOUR

THE WHORE OF REVELATION

Do you believe this monster is simply a backslidden or apostate church like many of our Christian leaders tell us, or is she the whore of Revelation? Let's look at scripture and check it out for ourselves. We find in chapter 17 of the Book of Revelation the Bible says, "I will show unto thee the judgment of the great whore that sitteth upon many waters:" And, of course, in scripture the reference to many waters means multitudes of people. Today the Vatican boasts over one billion followers. What's that, almost a quarter of the earth's population?

And it says, "With whom the kings of the earth have committed fornication." If you look back in history you will see that almost every king has had political, economic or religious ties with the Vatican, starting with Constantine the Great, who was actually the first pope, and presided over the first council. Constantine was never saved. (That was another smokescreen.) Most nations today have diplomatic representatives in the Vatican.

"And the inhabitants of the earth have been made drunk with the wine of her fornication." We have just looked at the madness of World War II and how it was set up by the Jesuits. And the Bible goes on to say, "The woman was arrayed in purple and scarlet." These are the official colors of the Vatican. "And decked with gold and precious stones and pearls," Did you know the Vatican is the wealthiest organization on the face of the earth? Later in the book I'll go into this in more detail. The Bible goes on to say, "And on her forehead was a name written, MYSTERY, BABYLON THE GREAT." Where did Catholicism come from? If you do a little research you'll find it came from the ancient

"...Babylon the great is fallen, is fallen, and is become the habitation of devils, and the hold of every foul spirit and a cage of every unclean and hateful bird." Rev. 18:2

Babylonian mysteries, and you can trace it right back to Nimrod and Semiramis. Only the names were changed to make it look like a Christian organization.

"The Mother of Harlots and Abominations of the earth." Can I name a few abominations that came from Rome? We have the Nazi Party, which was staffed with Jesuits and high ranking Catholics. And then we have the communist party, another offshoot, or branch of the mother of harlots. Listen to these names: Marx, Engels, Stalin, Lenin, Fidel Castro. All were trained and guided by Jesuits.

So these are her babies. Just a few of them, not to mention some of the spirit cults like voodoo. In the voodoo creed they state that, along with their religion of demon possession, they believe in "the holy Roman Catholic church."

The Bible goes on to say, "And I saw the woman drunken with the blood of the saints." The Roman Catholic Institution tortured, maimed and murdered 68 million people during the Spanish Inquisition alone, and many of these were Bible-believing Christians.

Who would ***you*** say the whore of Revelation is? Is it something that will come in the future, or are we stuck with it right now? Beloved, it is obvious the whore of Revelation is the Roman Catholic Institution, and God ***hates*** it! He wants His people to come out of it so that His love can be manifested. God says, "If you love me, keep my commandments." John 14:15

The New Book of Martyrs

Representation of the tortures used in the Inquisition.

At the end of the Dark Ages, when the popes ruthlessly controlled Europe, God raised up Christian men and women who knew the Bible and loudly proclaimed that the deadly Roman Catholic Institution was the whore of Revelation.

CHAPTER FIVE

ANOTHER GOSPEL

As a Christian, what do I do concerning the whore of Revelation? I'm accused of not showing love and of being too harsh exposing Catholicism. Am I being unscriptural? Let's see.

Bible Christianity and Roman Catholicism are doctrinally as far apart as the east is from the west. One is based on the Bible and the other on the traditions of men. So how can we walk together without compromise? It's impossible.

Many Protestants and Charismatic Catholics claim that the Holy Spirit is drawing them together. But, is it the Holy Spirit of God? Or could it be a different spirit? Are Charismatic Catholics leaving the whore of Revelation? Or are they being used to pull Protestants to Rome?

Some Charismatic Catholics claim that after being baptized by the Holy Spirit they have a deeper relationship with Mary, they can recite the rosary in tongues, and so on. None of this is in the Bible. They are the inventions of men. In 2 Corinthians 11:2-4, it says: "For I am jealous over you with godly jealousy: for I have espoused you to one husband, that I may present you as a chaste virgin to Christ. But I fear, lest by any means, as the serpent beguiled Eve through his subtlety, so your minds should be corrupted from the simplicity that is in Christ. For if he that cometh preacheth another Jesus, whom we have not preached, or if ye receive another spirit, which ye have not received, or another gospel, which ye have not accepted, ye might well bear with him." Paul is warning them here against following anyone preaching another gospel.

And then in John 16:13 it says: "Howbeit when he, the Spirit of truth, is come, he will guide you ***into all truth:*** for he shall not speak of himself; but whatsoever he shall hear, that shall he speak."

Now, God the Holy Spirit is the spirit of truth. How can He lead someone deeper into error? That's impossible, Beloved. That's a different spirit, and it is not from God. Satan is the master deceiver and this is his clever religious game to pull Protestants under the control of the whore.

Has Rome changed? Beloved, when the whore of Revelation dumps the mass, the veneration (or worship) of Mary, when they throw away their rosaries and repent from claiming that Mary was free from original sin just like Jesus, when they admit they cooked up the idea of purgatory; and when the priests of Rome concede to the priesthood of all believers; when the whore of Revelation does all that, then I will believe she is changing. People say she is changing, but, beloved, she is only changing her tactics.

How does a harlot, or whore, seduce her victims? The book of Proverbs tells us in chapter 7, verses 6 through 10: "I discerned among the youths, a young man void of understanding, Passing through the street near her corner; and he went the way to her house, In the twilight, in the evening, in the black and dark night: And behold, there met him a woman with the attire of a harlot, and subtil of heart." Then, verses 22 and 24 through 27: "With her much fair speech she caused him to yield, with the flattering of her lips she forced him. He goeth after her straightway, as an ox goeth to the slaughter. Hearken unto me now therefore, O ye children, and attend to the words of my mouth. Let not thine heart decline to her ways, go not astray in her paths. For she hath cast down many wounded: yea, many strong men have been slain by her. Her house is the way to hell, going down to the chambers of death."

The Bible says the mother of harlots will seduce kings and nations with her cunning; that the nations have been made drunk, which means they are confused, disoriented, unstable, and can be easily deceived and conquered by her.

Today, the whore has beguiled and flattered our Christian leaders into believing that she is part of the true body of Christ, and is simply a back-slidden or apostate church.

Rex[1] meets the Pope

"And what a dynamic moment it was for me as I finally greeted Pope John Paul II personally. It was clear that he had heard about our ministry. I shared with him our vision for the next three years – to take the gospel message by way of television into every nation on earth.

"As we talked together, I sensed more and more that our mission is the same: to build the body of Christ; to uplift our brethren in the Lord; to win the world for the kingdom; to share that shining message that Jesus gave us to share… 'You are loved.'

"I wish you could have been there, standing by my side, as I shared those few moments with Pope John Paul II. For those were milestone moments in my own personal life, in my spiritual life…"

[1]Rex Humbard, famous Evangelist
THE ANSWER, March 1980

I was shocked at being accused of dividing the brethren. They referred to the scripture which says, "Mark those which cause divisions among you and avoid them." But, beloved, why did they leave out the middle of the verse? Is there something wrong with it? Why don't they quote the whole thing? It says, "Now I beseech you, mark those which cause divisions and offences ***contrary to the doctrine which ye have learned*** and avoid them." This verse is found at the end of Romans, the great book on salvation by faith, not works. It's telling us to avoid those who teach anything other than salvation by faith in Christ alone. It is a warning against cults. A cult is anything that takes away from the sufficiency of Christ's sacrifice on Calvary.

I'm causing a division all right, but not between brethren. We need to be specific about the different kinds of division. We must not create division between our brethren in Christ; those who hold to the true gospel that we are saved by faith, and faith alone. But the Bible says we must separate from those teaching false doctrine — another gospel. It's a division between the saved and the lost.

Jesus said in Matt. 10:34, "Think not that I am come to send peace on earth, I came not to send peace, but a sword. For I am come to set a man at variance against his father and the daughter against her mother and the daughter-in-law against her mother-in-law. And a man's foes shall be they of his own household. He that loveth father or mother more than me is not worthy of me. He that loveth son or daughter more than me is not worthy of me. And he that taketh not his cross and followeth after me is not worthy of me. He that findeth his life shall lose it, and he that loseth his life for my sake shall find it." Jesus is talking here about separation. We must take a stand for the gospel no matter the cost.

I'd like to quote a dear brother in Christ. I think this will help to put things in their proper perspective. He said, "Because we live at a time when terms like love and unity are so appealing, it is quite difficult to argue that these words have been taken out of context and do not mean what we think they mean. Love without truth is whoredom. To compromise is to reject the gospel, and without the gospel there is no hope. In a choice between unity and truth, unity must yield to truth, for it is far better to be divided by truth than to be united by error."

In His Word, God says that Truth is all-important, that we should depart from those who hold not the truth. God said that we should examine everything carefully, and hold fast to that which is good, and reject that which is evil. Dare we set aside what God says?

Some say we are standing on the brink of the end of the Protestant era, and we will see the birth of the superchurch. Beloved, that superchurch has always been here. As God's people, we are to oppose her and tell the Roman Catholics to come out of her in obedience to Christ.

The Bible tells us in Ephesians 5:11: "And have no fellowship with the unfruitful works of darkness, but rather reprove them." Reprove means to express disapproval of, to rebuke, to expose it for what it is. Christ tells us in the Book of Revelation, chapter 18, verses 6 and 7 concerning the mother of harlots to "Reward her even as she rewarded you, and double unto her double according to her works: in the cup which she hath filled fill to her double. How much she hath glorified herself, and lived deliciously, so much torment and sorrow give her:"

That's the only place in scripture we are told to fight back. It is our responsibility. She has betrayed the Catholic people. She is destroying Protestantism. And by God's grace we will rip the self-righteous robes off that whore and expose her filthy running sores, her lies, crimes, the blood that is on her hands and her murderous intentions against God's people. When we expose her, and the Catholic people see what she has done, and the world sees, they're going to flee from her and turn to Christ.

What kind of warfare are Christians to be in? It's a spiritual war! We're not to pick up weapons and go after the Catholic people. You must understand what's involved here. We are locked into a spiritual warfare over the souls of men. The Bible says, "For we wrestle not against flesh and blood, but against principalities, against powers, against the rulers of the darkness of this world, against spiritual wickedness in high places." Ephesians 6:12

The Bible explains it in Ephesians 6. If we follow this through and arm ourselves and fight the spiritual warfare, then we'll be victorious. But Christ has to go before us.

Beloved, we ***are*** in a spiritual warfare. Be on the offensive. Never give in. Satan ***hates*** prayer. Take authority over occult powers in the name of our Lord. Assault the gates of hell, and he will fall back. Satan can only harm us if God gives him the authority, so he bluffs, lies and threatens, etc. Regardless of his technique to confuse, if the Lord Jesus is lifted up, Satan is damaged. And when we've done all, we must have the guts to stand. We cannot stand on our own… it's only through the grace and power of God. Always send the Lord before you into battle.

Am I wrong in exposing the whore? No! I'm being obedient to the Word of God. Our position might not be the popular one but we are not to please men. In Galatians 1:10 it says: "For do I now persuade men or God? or do I seek to please men? for if I yet pleased men, I should not be a servant of Christ."

CHAPTER SIX

COVER UP

When World War II ended, the Vatican had egg all over its face. Pope Pius XII, after building the Nazi war machine, saw Hitler losing his battle against Russia, and he immediately jumped to the other side as he saw the handwriting on the wall. General Eisenhower saved his neck. Pope Pius XII should have stood before the judges in Nuremburg. His war crimes were worthy of death. But the Vatican was pulling every string she could, and Pope Pius XII came out smelling like a rose.

Too many people knew that the Vatican was responsible for World War II so it was time for a face lift. Time to start up smokescreens. The Vatican II Council came into existence and the mother of harlots put on a new make-up job. She wiped her mouth with her bloody hands and said, "I've changed. Now I like the Protestants. I'm not going to call them heretics any more, but separated brethren." She told the Protestants to forget the past. It was now time to push the love gospel. A time of healing. Just like in France and Ireland. Remember…?

Catholic Twin Circle, October 11,1981

Bishop Fulton J. Sheen

There were so many books in the gospel book stores exposing the whore that the Vatican had to create a common enemy for both Catholics and Protestants to unite against. Bishop Fulton J. Sheen launched the anti-communist attack, and behold, like mushrooms, we saw anti-communist ministries popping up exposing the monster in Moscow.

The Jesuits were busy on many fronts. The John Birch Society blossomed, aided by the Jesuits, because it served their purpose to have attention of the Protestants shifted from the Vatican to Communism. At this time, Senator McCarthy was riding high. Publishers stopped publishing books exposing the whore and turned their attention to Communism. Some Christian publishers were bought out, others didn't want to make a stand because it would raise eyebrows.

So the Vatican was succeeding in their goals. Their boys, planted in Protestant denominations, frowned on anti-Catholic sermons and discouraged them across the nation. We were locked into a cold war with Russia. Hollywood, influenced by a powerful Catholic lobby, furnished us with films like "Song of Bernadette" and "Going My Way," and a number of exciting films glorifying the Catholic faith. On the other hand, they pushed movies like "Elmer Gantry" showing crooked Protestant evangelists. Do you remember "Dragnet" on television? The Christian was always pictured with a big Bible, smiling after he had strangled Grandma up in the attic. And always, the priests were the good guys. Just like in the popular television series called MASH. You see, we are hit psychologically on many fronts.

Fifty years of the movies

ABOVE: Ingrid Bergman and Bing Crosby in "The Bells of St. Mary's," the popular sequel to "Going My Way."

LEFT: Bill Christopher, who plays "Father Mulcahy" on the ever popular television program "MASH".

Our Sunday Visitor
April 5,1981

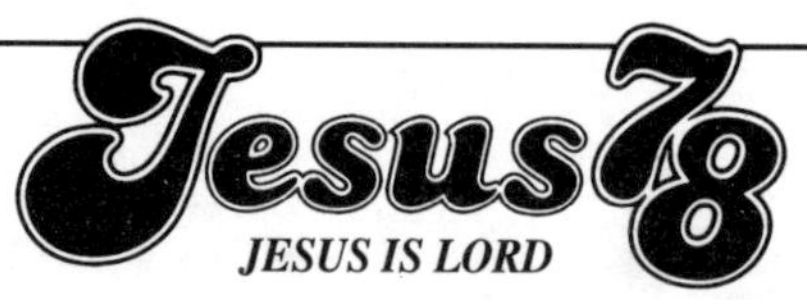

A DAY IN MAY AT THE MEADOWLANDS

Saturday, May 13, 1978 9:00 a.m.–4:30 p.m.

Route #3, N.J. Turnpike - 76,800 seats •Acres of parking

GIANTS STADIUM — SPORTS COMPLEX

Ruth Carter Stapleton

Jim Bakker

Father John Bertolucci

Father Michael Scanlan

"THAT ALL MAY BE ONE"
John 17:21
Admission by Ticket only
Children to 13 – Free
Youth – 13 to 18–$1.00
Adult Groups
(10 or more) $2.50
Individual $3.50

MUSIC
WITNESS
FELLOWSHIP

Andrae Crouch

Please call from 10-12 a.m. and 2-4 p.m.
Contact: People of Hope,
Xavier Center, Convent Station, N.J. 07961
(201) 267-0617
or
Logos International, Box 191,
Plainfield, N.J. 07061, (201) 754-0745

CHAPTER SEVEN

SHOW BIZ

Do I dare talk about ***Christian*** television? I think I'd better. Let us take a look at what has happened to our Christian television networks. We have Jim Bakker, on PTL; you have 700 Club with Pat Robertson, and the biggie here on the West Coast is Paul and Jan Crouch with their TBN. They all have something in common. They all have nuns and priests on their programs.

I have watched Paul and Jan on Channel 40, and sometimes, I feel so heavy hearted. I watch all these nuns and priests coming on. Once I heard Paul and Jan saying, "Oh, I don't understand the mass, but it's very interesting." God has warned us as Christians to have nothing to do with the works of darkness.

They have a priest that they're sponsoring on their network program. His name is Manning. He wistfully looks at the Protestants and begs for funds to sponsor Catholic missionaries. Christians are depriving their own pastors and their own churches by sending their money in to TBN for this priest. Those dear little old grandmothers send him love offerings and it is only making the Vatican wealthier. There's going to be a lot to give an account for, beloved.

We've ended up with Christian show business. We have a bunch of new stars singing snappy little songs and swinging hymns, beating drums, wearing sequins, and telling us how good Jesus is. We can watch a variety of speakers and singers for hours on end. So who reads the Bible when they can watch Christian television? It looks like it has replaced the Word of God for many. They're looking at people instead of going to the Bible for answers, and getting their noses into history to find out what's going on.

Some people have Channel 40 and PTL on like a rabbit's foot. They figure God's going to bless them because they have this holy program on. I have a friend whose Dad is an unsaved Roman Catholic. This man goes to mass, beats his wife, swears like a sailor, drinks his booze, but he watches Christian television every night. The house is filled with statues of saints and the Virgin Mary, and the crucifix. He gets blind drunk. He sits there with his cigar and his booze, with his feet up on the chair, and he watches Paul and Jan. He is convinced, after watching the Catholics on that network, that he is on his way to heaven. When his son-in-law tries to witness to him, he points to the smiling priests and nuns on those Christian stations and says, "See? We're all Christians." I believe this man's blood is going to be on their hands.

The Vatican now has a satellite and soon the pope will be able to speak to every Roman Catholic on the face of this earth at the same time. Beloved, if you play footsies with the Vatican, you lose. I believe in the future you will see that our Christian television heroes with giant ministries will soon be picked off one by one. All of the biggies will fall for one reason or another. And the last hero alive will be his holiness in the Vatican, and the world will love him.

News

OurSundayVisitor

Get ready America, here comes national Catholic TV

By Charles A. Savitskas

A national Catholic television network is no longer a dream. A vast telecommunications network is already rapidly taking shape within the Church and the U.S. planners say that between fall and next January, some 75 major dioceses will be utilizing the *Westar* communications satellite through a series of earth stations.

Technical plans have been no problem and, in fact, are well advanced. The estimated 75 diocesan earth stations, called downlinks, will get most of their broadcast material, via satellite, from one or two program distribution points, called uplinks. One of those uplinks will certainly be in New York. If a second is built, it will be on the West Coast, possibly San Francisco or Los Angeles. The uplinks will be operated by the newly incorporated National Catholic Telecommunications Network. And the satellite owned by Western Union will be leased, at first, for five hours a day, five days a week.

Next year, however, additional time will be sought on the new RCA satellite, and within two to three years, planners hope to be using a satellite round-the-clock.

The technical consultant, Satellite System Engineering, in Washington, DC, has been working since last September on design specifications for the earth stations, both the uplinks and downlinks. They have also been evaluating bidders for constructing the system. At this point Microwave and quality program material, for which the system has a voracious appetite.

Success depends on the quality of the programming. The cost will take care of itself, if the quality of the programming is good. For the first time, the Church will be competing with network stations for the viewers' time. If the Church provides a good alternative home video environment, there will be no problem.

The magnititude of the plan, according to Father Michael J. Dempsey, a Brooklyn priest who is the satellite project director, can easily be compared to the bishops' decision last century when they agreed to build a Catholic school system. They opted for the system in order to educate the large Catholic immigration after the 1840s, but "without knowing the problems it would represent. But they built it as a way of being Church to this new world of people which had suddenly swelled to 10 million in 10 years." The satellite system, by comparison, is the most adventuresome and certainly the most costly undertaking the bishops have ever embarked upon.

Unlike the school system, however, the enormous cost of the system is intended to

The project is in the uncommonly comfortable position of having top level approval.

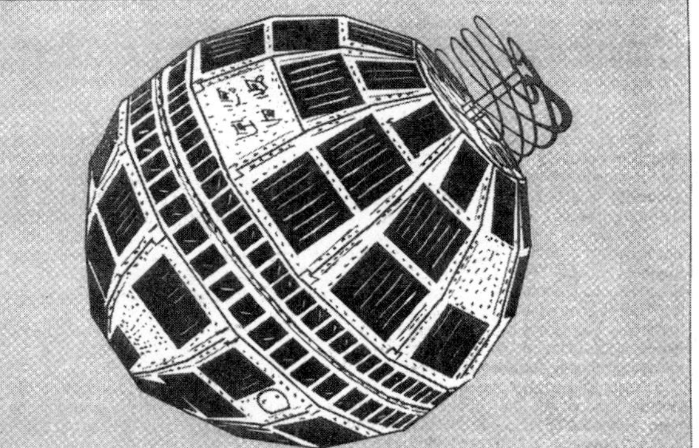

gets income from both Protestant and Catholic viewers, and is "eminently successful economically." Its annual income is roughly between $300 and $500 million. For Father Dempsey, such examples offer reassurance that the communication satellite project will not be taking money from CCD or schools or the parish. In fact, if there were any sign that it would threaten the satellite. These can be redistributed locally to cover all the cable systems and institutions in the area. Then, later, it can gradually move to electronics as it gets the capital and receives income to do that.

Above all, says Father Dempsey, individual dioceses should get "actively involved in the franchising process of the local cable systems." The cable systems

OUR SUNDAY VISITOR, April 26, 1981

The Bible says, in II Corinthians 6:14, "Be ye not unequally yoked together with unbelievers: for what fellowship hath righteousness with unrighteousness? and what communion hath light with darkness? And what concord hath Christ with Belial? or what part hath he that believeth with an infidel?" and then in verse 17 it goes on to say, "Wherefore come out from among them, and be ye separate, saith the Lord, and touch not the unclean thing; and I will receive you, And will be a Father unto you, and ye shall be my sons and daughters, saith the Lord Almighty."

CHAPTER EIGHT

THE FALLEN IDOL

The Vatican always looks and plans way into the future, from 25, to 50, to 100 years in advance. After World War II, the Vatican had to pick and back an American champion who would be a friend, a man they would help put on a pedestal, who would be loved by everybody. God forbid that he should ever be a Martin Luther! This champion would woo and win the hearts of the American people, a biggie, a champion they would support. He could be used as the pied piper who would pull all the evangelicals into the arms of the pope.

They wanted a man who would be a good speaker, a man with charisma who could pack stadiums; a man who would preach a gospel message, but on the soft side; one who would ***never*** attack the Vatican. And so when they found him, William Randolph Hearst, a good Roman Catholic publisher, used his newspaper chain to push Billy Graham to fame.

For 30 years, Billy Graham spoke to multitudes and became greatly loved, respected, and imitated. When he preached, he was honored and men praised him. Yet when Jesus Christ preached, they killed Him.

I often read the scripture: "Whosoever, therefore, will be a friend of the world is the enemy of God." The newspapers never really blasted Billy Graham. Magazines said he was one of the world's most loved men. Somehow, I kept getting a "tilt" sign flashing in my mind. I've loved Billy, prayed for him and supported him. But I sensed something was wrong.

Oakland Bishop Floyd begin chats with Billy Graham
They discuss Jesuit's book lauding Graham's ministry

Oakland Tribune, July 29, 1971

Belmont Abbey College
Belmont, North Carolina

March 19, 1965

Mr. Julius C. Taylor
100 Cardinal Drive
Taylors, South Carolina

Dear Mr. Taylor:

Your very nice letter addressed to the Rev. John Oetgen has been handed to me for reply. Father John is no longer president and is at the University of North Carolina working on his dissertation for the doctorate in Literature.

I am the one who, being acquainted with Billy Graham, invited him to speak to the Fathers, the Nuns, students and invited guests, and I am pleased to reply to your inquiries.

Billy Graham gave an inspiring and a theologically sound address that may have been given by Bishop Fulton J. Sheen or any other Catholic preacher. I have followed Billy Graham's career and I must emphasize that he has been more Catholic than otherwise, and I say this not in a partisan manner but as a matter of fact.

Knowing the tremendous influence of Billy Graham among Protestants and now the realization and acknowledgment among Catholics of his devout and sincere appeal to the teachings of Christ which he alone preaches, I would state that he could bring Catholics and Protestants together in a healthy ecumenic spirit.

I was the first Catholic to invite Billy Graham; I know he will speak at three other Catholic universities next month; I believe he will be invited by more Catholic colleges in the future than Protestant colleges.

So I am well pleased, then, to answer your question: Billy Graham is preaching a moral and evangelical theology most acceptable to Catholics.

With cordial regards, I remain

Very sincerely yours,

Cuthbert E. Allen, OSB

(The Rev.) Cuthbert E. Allen, O.S.B.
Executive Vice-President

CEA:mc

Billy Graham and the Church of Rome

Billy Graham at Roman Catholic Belmont College receiving the yoke from ROME. Graham was granted an honorary doctor's degree from this Roman Catholic College. Graham told his audience that the 'GOSPEL THAT FOUNDED THIS COLLEGE IS THE SAME GOSPEL WHICH I PREACH TODAY.'

I was told that when Anita Bryant spoke out against homosexuals and asked for Billy's support, he turned her down. He played it cool. Anita Bryant took the heat and was persecuted for her stand, but not Billy. He was loved by the world for his position.

Billy Graham began his ministry as a fundamentalist, and as time passed, he changed his position. Listen to this: In the Catholic Herald of June 3, 1966, Billy Graham is quoted as being a friend of the Jesuits in the United States. Here's another one: Dr. Billy Graham received an honorary degree of Doctor of Humane Letters from the Roman Catholic College, Belmont Abbey, in 1967. Billy noted the significance of the occasion by saying that this is "a time when Catholics and Protestants could meet together and greet each other as brothers, whereas 10 years ago, they could not."

In April, 1972, Billy Graham received the International Franciscan Award in Minneapolis, given by the Franciscan Friars for true ecumenism. Before I quote what Billy Graham said about Francis of Assissi, first let me say this about St. Francis. He believed he was saved by works, by helping the poor. This way, he believed he was saving his soul. St. Francis was canonized, which means he was made a saint by the Roman Catholic Institution because of his strong position on the doctrine of works. Beloved, we know that this is unscriptural. Did you know that St. Francis of Assissi blessed and baptized animals and gave them Christian names?

Now, what did Billy Graham say about this strange fellow? He said, "While I am not worthy to touch the shoe laces of St. Francis, yet this same Christ that called Francis in the 13th century also called me to be one of His servants in the 20th century."

When Billy Graham appeared on the Phil Donahue Show of October 11, 1979, in discussing Pope John Paul II's visit to the United States of America, Billy Graham said, "I think the American people are looking for a leader, a moral and spiritual leader that believes something. And he (meaning the pope) does. He didn't mince words on a single subject. As a matter of fact, his subject in Boston was really an evangelistic address in which he asked the people to come to Christ, to give their lives to Christ. I said, 'Thank God I've got somebody to quote now with some real authority.*'" How tragic. A man who once used the Bible as his authority is now putting the pope up on a pedestal and looking to him.

In the beginning, Billy Graham was greatly used of God, but I believe Billy gave in to tremendous pressures and compromised. And he is now walking hand in hand with the whore of Revelation.

A few years ago, 5 pastors from Mexico came to see me, asking for help. They told me I must talk to Billy Graham. I told them that was impossible, I was just a little tract publisher. Then they told me Billy Graham had destroyed their churches. They said he held a crusade, and told all those who had received Christ to go back to their original churches and win those people to Christ. The pastors told me their people followed Billy's instruction and all went back to the Roman Catholic system. Twelve years of work destroyed in one night.

Dr. Rivera, the ex-Jesuit priest, told me he knew Billy was being used by the Vatican in 1950 when the word came to all the Jesuits in Central and South America telling them to fill the stadiums with Roman Catholics whenever Billy Graham spoke. Millions were spent to promote Billy Graham as the world's greatest evangelist.

*October 11, 1979. Transcript #10119.

FAITH FOR THE FAMILY, Nov., 1982

The Religious News Service reported on January 13, 1981, "Pope John Paul II was closeted for almost two hours with the Rev. Billy Graham, the world's best-known Protestant evangelist."

"Following the New England Crusade, thousands of those who came forward are now in the process of being integrated into the Catholic church. Meetings have taken place between the Graham Association and Catholic clergy for the transfer of these people to the Roman church. One such meeting took place at Pope John XXIII Seminary in Weston, Massachusetts, on the evening of June 9, 1982, when the names of 2100 inquirers were given to priests and nuns."

‘THE POPE IS ALMOST AN EVANGELIST’

IN this exclusive interview, evangelist Billy Graham hails Pope John Paul II's pilgrimage to Poland as a triumph for Christianity. Dr. Graham and other religious leaders also heap praise on the pontiff for helping to push forward the religious revival worldwide.

The Star, June 26, 1979

Rome gives nothing to anybody unless you pay it off. Could it be that his final pay-off was to introduce Pope John Paul II as the greatest moral leader of the world? Which he did. Didn't he realize when he did this he was giving the whore a cloak of respectability? And all of Billy's followers, the evangelicals and multitudes of others across this land who listen to his every word, heard this endorsement, and trusting Billy, turned and gave their love to the communist from Poland dressed in his papal robes, who claims to be the representative of Christ on this earth. I can picture the pope smiling to himself, flying back victoriously to Rome. He knew that Billy had been a good investment.

It's a deadly game, beloved. And now that his work is over, he's no longer needed. I believe the Vatican set Billy up when he went to Russia. Believers in Christ go to our Lord for guidance and to the scriptures, and pray that God, the Holy Spirit, will lead us in all truth. But Billy admitted that he sought advice from Vatican officials about his trip to Russia. They told him to go quietly and not to criticize the communists' practices. And when he followed their instructions, the suffering brothers and sisters rotting in Russia's prisons who got 5 to 10 years for passing out a single gospel tract, were crushed when Billy announced to the world that there was religious freedom in Russia. Yes, beloved, Billy Graham, as much as I love him and hate to say it, I believe was cleverly used as a smokescreen and as a pied piper for the whore of Revelation.

CHAPTER NINE

BETRAYED?

When a Catholic plot is discovered or exposed, Rome calls upon specialists to solve the problem. These are men who are called ***truth distorters.*** They spearhead attacks to counter those who are trying to warn others. In WW II, when the Vatican was massacring the Greek Orthodox church members in Yugoslavia, survivors tried to reach the United States to tell of the murders with documented evidence. Once the information started coming in about what was happening in Yugoslavia, the master truth distorters moved against it, calling it anti-Catholic propaganda, and bigotry! They minimized the atrocities to confuse the public.

Such a man was Louis Adamic. His job was to convince the American people that the reports of the horrible massacres in Yugoslavia were not true. Adamic and the Catholic lobby working with him convinced President Roosevelt and his wife, Eleanor, that these massacres, the worst crimes of WW II, were only propaganda. Adamic persuaded Mrs. Roosevelt that these reports were false. When she discovered they were true, it was too late. Almost one million people had already met a ghastly death.

The Jesuits saw this as a critical area in the Christian community that would help the Vatican. They needed a group of experts to investigate cults, but they must never discuss Rome as an enemy. This would be another smokescreen. There are men in the Christian community, men who are highly trusted, loved, and respected. I believe that these men, either knowingly or unknowingly are doing the same job for the Vatican as Louis Adamic did. These men are dulling the eyes and ears of the

Christian believers, assuring them that the Pope is our friend. Their job is to play it down, ridicule and destroy the reputation of anyone trying to sound the alarm.

They tell concerned Christians that it is a lie, a joke, unreliable, that the material and evidence is a hoax and should be discarded as junk.

The Jesuits would need someone in a critical position to protect them in Protestant circles. If a person could be found, he could rise to a position of trust, as a watch-dog to protect the Protestants from the cults. A man who would join the ranks of those exposing the Biblical errors of the Jehovah's Witnesses, Mormons, Moonies and Eastern religions, and yet never attack the Roman Catholic Institution as the whore of Revelation, but

ALBERTO, page 27, Published by Chick Publications

This I.D. card was issued by the Spanish government in Spain in 1967, under the rule of the Spanish dictator Franco. His security forces were equally as strict as the Gestapo had been in Germany. To obtain this document, Alberto had to supply birth certificate, identification papers and positive proof from his archdiocese of being a priest. Several security organizations were involved, similar to our CIA and FBI. The priest, Alberto Rivera, had to be approved by all of these organizations to receive this document. There was no way it could have been a forgery. There is no question he was a priest. What you see here is positive proof. This document was granted by a government that had pledged absolute submission to the pope through the concordat signed by the government of Spain and the Vatican.

only refer to this system as a "backslidden or apostate Christian church," which of course, is the line the Jesuits use. Such a person could be very valuable for the cause of Roman Catholicism. Such a man could be a perfect smokescreen. Anyone rising up trying to sound the alarm about the whore of Revelation, trying to warn the Christians of a new inquisition, could be easily shot down by this expert on the cults because so many would trust him.

One of the most difficult decisions I've faced since I've been a Christian publisher was after I heard Dr. Rivera's true story, saw all his documents, photos, I.D.'s, and letters proving that he was a Jesuit priest. When it finally dawned on me that we were being set up for another inquisition, I realized what a mess I'd be in if I sounded the alarm and the Christians wouldn't believe it. I could lose our business, our reputation and friends. If I printed Alberto's story, I would be going into a battle that would jeopardize my family and my own life.

I realized no other Christian publisher would hit this issue because they could go under, and business-wise, it would be a disaster for them. I went before the Lord in prayer and the thing I dreaded came to pass. I asked the Lord if I should attack the mother of harlots and abominations of the earth.

SPANISH

ARZOBISPADO
DE
MADRID-ALCALA
CANCILLERIA - SECRETARIA

Su Excelencia Reverendísima, el Señor Obispo Auxiliar y Vicario General de este Arzobispado, ha tenido a bien autorizar a D. Alberto Rivera Romero *Sacerdote que reside en esta Archidiócesis, para que pueda salir al extranjero por motivos de* su ministerio

Madrid, 14 *de* septiembre *de* 1967

EL CANCILLER - SECRETARIO.

M. Amo

ENGLISH

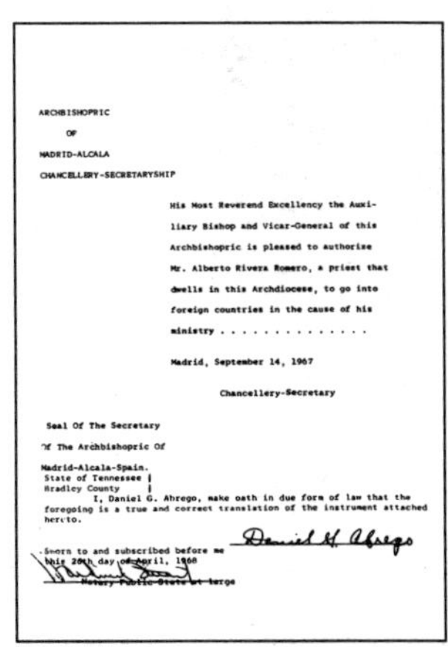

ARCHBISHOPRIC
OF
MADRID-ALCALA
CHANCELLERY-SECRETARYSHIP

His Most Reverend Excellency the Auxiliary Bishop and Vicar-General of this Archbishopric is pleased to authorize Mr. Alberto Rivera Romero, a priest that dwells in this Archdiocese, to go into foreign countries in the cause of his ministry . . . .

Madrid, September 14, 1967

Chancellery-Secretary

Seal Of The Secretary
Of The Archbishopric Of
Madrid-Alcala-Spain.

State of Tennessee |
Bradley County |

I, Daniel G. Abrego, make oath in due form of law that the foregoing is a true and correct translation of the instrument attached hereto.

Daniel G. Abrego

Sworn to and subscribed before me this 20th day of April, 1968

Notary Public State at large

This is a copy of the last official certification given to Alberto just before he left Spain in 1967.

Should I attack the Vatican? The Lord said yes. And so we published ALBERTO. I hoped, down in my heart, Walter Martin would back me up.

One thing stuck in my mind. Why didn't Walter Martin sound the alarm? He was the great expert on cults, especially since he knew all the history about the Inquisition. And yet he kept quiet. Why is Walter Martin defending this evil system, calling it a Christian church? The man is a genius. He knows about her history, and yet he's defending the whore of Revelation.

Beloved, the Bible tells us to seek the Lord in prayer. I go to prayer and get a specific answer from the Lord. I tell somebody I prayed about it and they say, "Oh, that's a cop-out." I really don't understand how they can say that. The Bible instructs us to seek the Lord for guidance. Have these people gotten so far off base that they can't understand a person trusting in Christ for guidance? If He is Lord, He must be the Lord of every part of our lives.

Letter after letter is coming in telling us how Roman Catholics have been saved through our material, and yet Christians sit around cracking their knuckles. The fields are white unto harvest and people are going to hell all around us. We've got 60 million Roman Catholics to be reached, and nobody wants to get involved. They're so afraid of what others will think of them, that they would rather sit back and watch people go to hell than risk offending them.

When the heat came on Chick Publications for what we were doing, I was amazed. It all came through the same group. There seemed to be a link between all these men who are promoting the story that Alberto is a fraud. Gary Metz had his article published in *Cornerstone*, *Christianity Today* and *Our Sunday Visitor*, a Catholic periodical. Brian Onken, Martin's research consultant, wrote an article that blasted us and defended the mother of cults. Then, you've got Bill Jackson in San Jose, and Bart Brewer in San Diego. Both of these men are supposed to be operating ministries to Catholics. And yet, they're going around to churches trying to destroy our credibility. Why? Doesn't that make you a little suspicious?

THE KINGDOM OF THE CULTS

An Analysis of the Major Cult Systems
in the Present Christian Era
by
WALTER MARTIN, M.A., PH.D.

CONTENTS

In Martin's KINGDOM OF THE CULTS he never mentions Roman Catholicism as a cult, and never tells lost Roman Catholics to come out of that unscriptural system "THE MOTHER OF HARLOTS AND ABOMINATIONS OF THE EARTH." (Rev. 17:5)

Does Walter Martin speak for the body of Christ? No! Only the Word of God does this. Yet, this man stands on his pedestal, with both hands filled with the slanderous garbage supplied by the Vatican and pro-Catholic sources, and he throws it at Alberto's character to destroy his reputation. Dr. Rivera says he has copies of the original material sent to Martin by the Vatican and the Jesuit superiors in Spain. But you'll notice, Martin hasn't bothered to attack Alberto's message that the Vatican is the whore of Revelation. Only Alberto, the man. And yet, is Martin without sin? What about Martin's past? His reputation could be slanderously destroyed also, just like anyone else's. Would this discredit all his information on Mormonism, and Jehovah's Witnesses? No! God uses us in spite of ourselves.

Who is really worthy to be used of God? Look in the Bible. Moses was a murderer. David was an adulterer. And yet, God used them in spite of their human failings. Our job is not to dig up dirt on any man. The Lord will take care of that because we will all give an account on the day of judgment. God knows the heart. We don't. Our job is to lift up Christ and evangelize the lost.

The Catholic controlled news media picked up the campaign against us, even U.S. News and World Report. We were blasted world-wide. Christianity Today did wonders for the Vatican. Their article was reprinted in Europe, Australia, etc. I couldn't believe the extent of the money spent to silence us. Before the book, **ALBERTO**, even got into Germany, the message was plastered all over Germany, France, South America, Mexico, Canada, into Asia, and England. What was so important about our comic **ALBERTO**, that this group would go to such lengths to try to discredit it?

The sad thing is all this money and energy was spent to stop this soulwinning comic book. And yet we have all these adult book stores and garbage like that and nobody says a word. But when we spoke out against Rome, all hell broke loose. A man once told me, "Jack, if you throw a rock down a dark alley and you hear a yell, you'll know you hit something." Well, from the sound of the scream that was let loose, I think we hit something big.

FROM A PORTION OF THE ARTICLE TITLED:

Tremors of Bigotry That Worry America

was arrested in the murder of three Laotians killed by arson in a northwestern suburb of Chicago. Since then, another Laotian community has been frightened by a series of fires set at their homes.

In a third Chicago suburb, the house of an immigrant family from India was pelted by rocks and BB's. The lawn was torn up by marauding cars, and the family's car was set afire.

Hispanic children in Cleveland schools complain they are frequently beaten up because of their ancestry.

Friction has also sparked violence against whites in places such as Miami, where several whites were among the 18 persons killed in ghetto riots last year. Members of a black-militant group called Alkebu-lan were blamed for the 22 stab wounds inflicted on James Earl Ray, convicted in the slaying of Martin Luther King, Jr., at a Tennessee prison in early June.

On the Gulf Coast of Texas, two Vietnamese, who claimed it was self-defense, were acquitted in the fatal shooting of a white man in a dispute over commercial-fishing rights.

Search for scapegoats. A main reason cited for the rise in bigotry is America's troubled economy. Cleveland lawyer Harry M. Brown, regional executive of a Jewish group called the Commission on Law and Public Affairs, explains by as the fact that they perceive it to be real."

Attacks on religious groups, though less violent, are also reported on the rise. The Catholic League for Religious and Civil Rights, for example, has become concerned about widespread sales of illustrated cartoon books that paint Catholicism in a bad light.

The books, published by the Los Angeles company of fundamentalist publisher Jack T. Chick, claim the Vatican has a "death list" and is conspiring to destroy Protestant churches by infiltrating them with Jesuit agents.

Divide and conquer. Another development worrying many theologians is the growing tendency of some believers to denigrate other religious groups. One example cited is a *New York* magazine interview in which an official of the fundamentalist Moral Majority was trying to back up his assertion that "Christians have never been anti-Semitic." When pressed to acknowledge anti-Semitism in the Spanish Inquisition, the preacher replied: "Those weren't Christians. They were Roman Catholics."

Nazis march on Jewish area in Southfield, Mich.

On June 2, Connecticut enacted a law banning paramilitary training camps of the kind opened by the Ku Klux Klan, from Illinois and Connecticut to Texas and Alabama. Similar legislation is pending in nearly a dozen other states.

Attempts by Klansmen and Nazis to win converts among students in high schools are meeting strong resistance from educators in several communities.

The New York City Police Department has formed a 14-member "bias-incident-investigation unit." Some black leaders in Detroit have called for the revival of a similar squad, which was disbanded with the ebbing of racial troubles in 1977.

U.S. NEWS & WORLD REPORT,
July 13, 1981,
Page 49

On the night of February 2,1982, I was watching Channel 40, the Trinity Broadcasting Network in Southern California. Harold Bredeson, a prominent ecumenical leader was talking to Walter Martin. Bredeson turned to the camera and he said something like this: "Walter Martin was the one who helped the charismatic movement to be accepted by the denominations by not attacking it." Walter hung his head and smiled. You see, beloved, Walter Martin calls the Roman Catholic Charismatics his brothers and sisters in Christ. These people still attend mass and worship that little Jesus cookie as God Almighty. Do you see the danger here? It looks like we have been betrayed, beloved!

The Apostle Paul said in II Timothy 4:14, "Alexander the coppersmith did me much evil: the Lord reward him according to his works." Beloved, I've seen the tremendous spiritual damage Walter Martin has done in discrediting our books exposing the whore of Revelation, in that precious Roman Catholics trusting wholeheartedly in Walter Martin have stayed in that system because he wouldn't tell them to come out. Martin's followers see no need to reach the Roman Catholic people. They look upon our soulwinning material with contempt. And I say, with a heavy heart, as Paul did, may the Lord reward Walter Martin according to his works.

The Bible says, "Cursed be the man that trusteth in man, and maketh flesh his arm, and whose heart departeth from the Lord." (Jer. 17:5) Think about it. Could this be another smokescreen to make Christians believe that the whore of Revelation is really a Christian group? Jesus says, "Come out of her, my people that ye be not partakers of her sins and that ye receive not of her plagues." (Rev. 18:4) Does Walter Martin tell them to come out? Not that I know of. Which one will ***you*** follow?

John Paul II, "Pilgrimage of Faith"

CHAPTER TEN

THE RICHEST MAN ON EARTH?

Remember when the pope came to the United States? How he chided us for not showing mercy? That we should give away what we have to the poor? We are such a wealthy nation. And then remember the great earthquake that took place in 1980 over in Italy? I remember when the pope came in to this ruined area, walked up to the bedside of some poor little wounded Italian man and the pope so benevolently laid his hand on his head and made the sign of the cross, blessed the man and walked off.

And the newscasters were telling of the devastation. And then we cut back to the United States and Senator Kennedy looked at the camera with sorrowful eyes and said, "Oh, we Americans, out of mercy we should send at least 45 million dollars to this devastated village so we can reconstruct it." Remember that? Now let me read something out of **THE VATICAN BILLIONS** by Avro Manhattan, and I think you're going to get as mad as I am right now. I want to bring to your attention the fact that this information was published 10 years ago, and the figures are probably even more startling today.

"The Vatican has large investments with the Rothschilds of Britain, France and America, with the Hambros Bank, with the Credit Suisse in London and Zurich. In the United States it has large investments with the Morgan Bank, the Chase-Manhattan Bank, the First National Bank of New York, the Bankers Trust Company, and others. The Vatican has billions of shares in the most powerful international corporations such as Gulf Oil, Shell, General Motors, Bethlehem Steel, General Electric, International Business Machines, T.W.A., etc. At a conservative estimate, these amount to more than 500 million dollars in the U.S.A. alone.

"In a statement published in connection with a bond prospectus, the Boston archdiocese listed its assets at Six Hundred and Thirty-five Million ($635,891,004), which is 9.9 times its liabilities. This leaves a net worth of Five Hundred and Seventy-one million dollars ($571,704,953). It is not difficult to discover the truly astonishing wealth of the church, once we add the riches of the twenty-eight archdioceses and 122 dioceses of the U.S.A., some of which are even wealthier than that of Boston.

"Some idea of the real estate and other forms of wealth controlled by the Catholic church may be gathered by the remark of a member of the New York Catholic Conference, namely 'that his church probably ranks second only to the United States Government in total annual purchase.' Another statement, made by a nationally syndicated Catholic priest, perhaps is even more telling. 'The Catholic church,' he said, 'must be the biggest corporation in the United States. We have a branch office in every neighborhood. Our assets and real estate holdings must exceed those of Standard Oil, A.T.&T., and U.S. Steel combined. And our roster of dues-paying members must be second only to the tax rolls of the United States Government.'

"The Catholic church, once all her assets have been put together, is the most formidable stockbroker in the world. The Vatican, independently of each successive pope, has been increasingly orientated towards the U.S. The Wall Street Journal said that the Vatican's financial deals in the U.S. alone were so big that very often it sold or bought gold in lots of a million or more dollars at one time.

"The Vatican's treasure of solid gold has been estimated by the United Nations World Magazine to amount to several billion dollars. A large bulk of this is stored in gold ingots with the U.S. Federal Reserve Bank, while banks in England and Switzerland hold the rest. But this is just a small portion of the wealth of the Vatican, which in the U.S. alone, is greater than that of the five wealthiest giant corporations of the country. When to that is added all the real estate, property, stocks and shares abroad, then the staggering accumulation of the wealth of the Catholic church becomes so formidable as to defy any rational assessment.

"The Catholic church is the biggest financial power, wealth accumulator and property owner in existence. She is a greater possessor of material riches than any other single institution, corporation, bank, giant trust, government or state of the whole globe. The pope, as the visible ruler of this immense amassment of wealth, is consequently the richest individual of the twentieth century. No one can realistically assess how much he is worth in terms of billions of dollars."

And I think back about how the pope, the wealthiest man on this planet, walked up to that poor little Italian man lying in that rubble, put his hand on his head, and said, "Bless you," and then walked away and just left him there. That has got to be the height of hypocrisy. And then Sen. Kennedy, the pope's boy over in the United States makes the big pitch to the U.S. people to foot the bill to repair that devastated village, right in the pope's backyard. What a set-up!

CHAPTER ELEVEN

Blueprint For Catholic America

I questioned Dr. Rivera about the briefings he received in the Vatican when he was a Jesuit priest. I asked him if he was briefed on how the Vatican planned to take over the United States. He told me his indoctrination went back to the time of the Pilgrims. Because of the knowledge of the Inquisition and the slaughter of Christians by the Roman Catholic system, the early immigrants in America began passing laws to keep Jesuits out of this country and to outlaw the mass...to protect themselves from a Vatican take-over. These were Christian communities deeply concerned about the whore of Revelation.

Jesuits began arriving in America as early as the second group of Pilgrims. They used different names with I.D.'s. They were followed years later when the Vatican sent multitudes of Catholic families from England, Ireland and France posing as Protestants, into the colonies. These were plants. They were holding secret masses in defiance of the laws. In those days, no Roman Catholic was to hold any position in civil government. The Jesuits made sure this part of our history was erased and removed.

The next major move by the Jesuits was to destroy or control all the Christian schools across America. Throughout the years, Jesuits, working undercover, have gotten into special committees on school boards to remove the emphasis of the Bible and replace it with psychology as found in the Spiritual Exercises of Ignatius de Loyola, the founder of the Jesuit Society. Later, Catholic schools and universities sprang up all across the nation under the Jesuits. Today, they probably outnumber all the Christian schools and colleges put together.

The third stage was to move into the courts and legislation, and branches of the judiciary to take over as judges and lawyers, in order to manipulate the Constitution in their favor until it could be changed. Once this was accomplished, the thrust was into politics to capture the political parties. Then the military and the newspapers. Even back in the times of Lincoln over half the newspapers in the United States were controlled by the Vatican.

I asked Dr. Rivera: What about the military picture today? How Catholic is our military position?

Dr. Rivera said: Horrifying.

I then asked about the political picture.

Dr. Rivera said: It is even worse.

Then I said: What about the Catholic structure in the judiciary?

Dr. Rivera shook his head and said: It is ***very*** painful because of the heavy Jesuit penetration in this area. Most of the judicial decisions are distorting and perverting the Constitution of the United States to take away our freedoms, preparing the way for anarchy for the final take-over of the United States.

Then I said: Is this preparing the way for the coming inquisition?

And Dr. Rivera said: That's correct. First for anarchy. We were briefed that after all these years of penetration and infiltration, what was needed was riots and anarchy in order to finally take over. By the time the Roman Catholic Institution is ready to take over politically, militarily, educationally, and religiously, that means they will have some legal basis to do so and this will be

Dr. Alberto Rivera (ex-Jesuit priest)

through the concordat which has already been prepared and that is being already negotiated. I see happening right now what I was told during those briefings back in the Vatican.

Then I said to him: Is the Vatican behind our present recession and economic situation, and is this leading us towards the coming riots?

Dr. Rivera said: Yes, that's correct, You can see right now that the Vatican is playing certain tricks with the economy. The world is going through an economic crisis and the Vatican would have us to believe that it is affecting them also. This is just a cover-up.

And then I said: What about the possibility of strikes? And how deeply are they involved in the unions?

Dr. Rivera replied: The Roman Catholic Institution has prepared that well, because the unions are led by the Jesuits in this country. What this means is the unions will never rest until they see that ***every*** industry in this country collapses.

Then I said: What do you see as a hope for the United States? A revival among the Christians and they actually start exposing Rome and pastors start preaching this from the pulpits, or is it already too late?

Dr. Rivera replied: It's never too late because it's in the hands of the Lord. What I believe with all my heart through the study of the scriptures plus my personal experience with the harlot is that, prophetically speaking, God is going to fulfill His prophecy, and He will allow these prophecies to take place in the United States. But it is a matter of time. What we are dealing with here is that God can either shorten or lengthen the time until these events take place. The Roman Catholic Institution is feeling the impact of your publications, and the message that God has given us

during these last days in the sense that they themselves know that if they carry out certain actions, people will immediately detect and will recognize what the Vatican is up to.
This is one of the dilemmas they face right now. If it were not for the publications we printed, we would be in a different situation today. What that means is the Lord has granted every Christian, pastor and church in the United States, without them even being aware of it, and even those who are opposing us, they are being preserved and the Lord is giving us more time in order that the Christians may respond.

If we act according to the will of God in these prophetical days against the tricks, programs and actions of the harlot in the United States, we will not be able to destroy her. We will not be able to stop her. But we will be able to do two things: First, to carry the message of the gospel to the lost Roman Catholic people. Second, we will have time enough for the Christian church to realize that her mission is here and now — not tomorrow. And God is just waiting for the church to act in order to restrain the forces of evil, the powers of darkness, the pope, the Jesuits and the Catholic institution from committing the crimes she is about to put into action the minute she completely takes over the United States.

Then I said: Now this is the information you received in the Vatican under the teachings of Augustin Cardinal Bea and the Jesuit General Pedro Arrupe?

And Dr. Rivera said: Yes, and also from the previous Jesuit General.

This excerpt from the tract MACHO (no longer in print) shows how communism ties in with the Vatican plan to take over the U.S.

READ "THE VATICAN MOSCOW WASHINGTON ALLIANCE" BY AVRO MANHATTAN, PUBLISHED BY CHICK PUBLICATIONS.

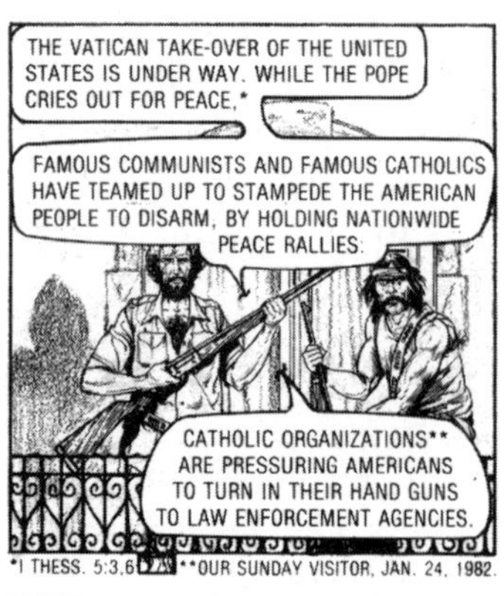

*I THESS. 5:3,6 **OUR SUNDAY VISITOR, JAN. 24, 1982.

*WALL STREET JOURNAL, JUNE 9, 1982
**"THE SECRET HISTORY OF THE JESUITS," PG. 156-157

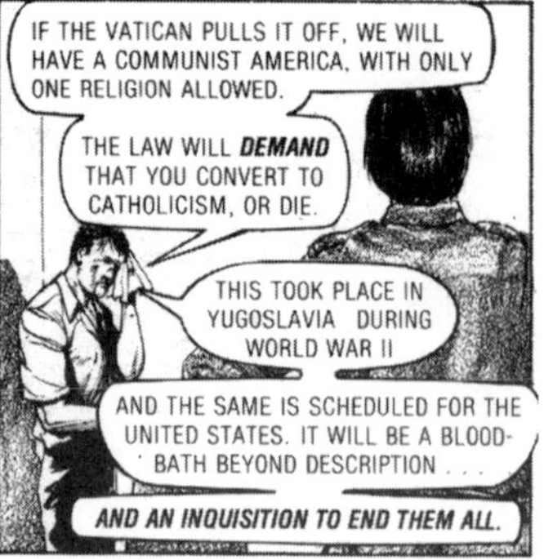

Currents in the News

Bishops, Brezhnev Fuel Nuclear Debate

Ronald Reagan's defense policy came under assault in late October from opposite directions: The threat of an intensified arms race by Russia's Leonid Brezhnev and a tilt toward antinuclear pacifism by the hierarchy of America's Roman Catholic Church.

Two days after a panel of U.S. Catholic bishops questioned the morality of nuclear weapons, Brezhnev said the Soviet Union must expand its arsenal even more. The U.S., he claimed, is threatening to "push the world into the flames of nuclear war."

One White House official speculated that Brezhnev wanted to do more than assure his generals that Moscow will keep pace in the arms race. The aide said the Soviet chief also hoped to fuel the drive in the U.S. for a freeze on nuclear weapons.

Defense Secretary Caspar Weinberger drew a direct link between American advocates of a freeze and Brezhnev's Kremlin speech. Stressing the Soviet leader's call for a stronger capability to wage war, Weinberger declared: "This would underline more than anything we could say the reasons for not entering into a freeze."

Weinberger and other officials tried to make a case for nuclear weapons with Catholic bishops wrestling with theological aspects of the arms race. The appeals had little impact on the bishops' five-man Committee on War and Peace, which on October 25 proposed a statement branding elements of U.S. nuclear strategy immoral. Examples—

First use. The U.S. has argued that nuclear weapons may be needed to halt a conventional attack. Said the bishops: "We find the moral responsibility of beginning nuclear war not justified by rational political objectives."

Civilian targets. America for years has targeted Soviet cities in the event of nuclear war—a policy the bishops said is wrong even if U.S. cities are hit first. Argued the clerics: "No Christian can rightfully carry out orders or policies deliberately aimed at killing noncombatants."

POKEMPNER—CLICK/CHICAGO; TIMOTHY A. MURPHY—USN&WR

Chicago's Bernardin heads bishops' committee. Weinberger says a freeze would hurt arms talks.

The committee, headed by Chicago's Archbishop Joseph L. Bernardin, said its position was rooted in Genesis. "The destructive potential of the nuclear powers threatens the sovereignty of God over the world He has brought into being," the bishops declared. "We could destroy His work."

Whether the document becomes church policy is up to the nearly 300 members of the National Conference of Catholic Bishops, which will debate it in mid-November and vote on it next spring. Reagan's aides are expected to keep reminding the bishops that a pacifist stance would weaken America's deterrent forces and undermine arms-control talks with Russia.

More in line with the administration's views was a letter sent months ago by New York's Cardinal Terence Cooke to Catholic chaplains in the military. For 15 centuries, he wrote, the church has taught that Catholics have "the right and the duty to protect its people against unjust aggression." □

U.S. NEWS & WORLD REPORT, Nov. 8, 1982, Page 15

Then I said: Were they very confident of taking over the United States?

And Dr. Rivera said: Very much so, very confident. They have the necessary influence to control either political party, regardless of whichever party is in power, and they will have their goals accomplished.

Then I said: So they now have the influence to control both political parties?

And Dr. Rivera said: Yes.

Then I said: They control our post office? And the media?

And Dr. Rivera said: Let's put it this way. The word control, I don't think is the proper word right now. I will say this. There is a very strong influence. There is a certain amount of control, but it is not absolute control in any of the areas. This is why we are still blessed by the fact that there are still men in the FBI, there are men in the CIA, men in the Congress, men in the Senate, men in the judicial system, men in every strata of life in the United States that still, many not even being Christians, are still Americans, that are still loyal to the principles of the Constitution as given from the beginning, not as it is now.

And then I said: Okay, who are the Knights of Columbus loyal to? Where does their loyalty stand? With the United States, or with the Vatican?

Dr. Rivera said: The Knights of Columbus have to give their loyalty to the pope. They cannot base it on the constitution of the United States because they would be destroyed by the Vatican if they did so, as others have been destroyed in the past.

Then I said: Will the Knights of Columbus play a vital part in the attack against the Christians when the U.S. falls?

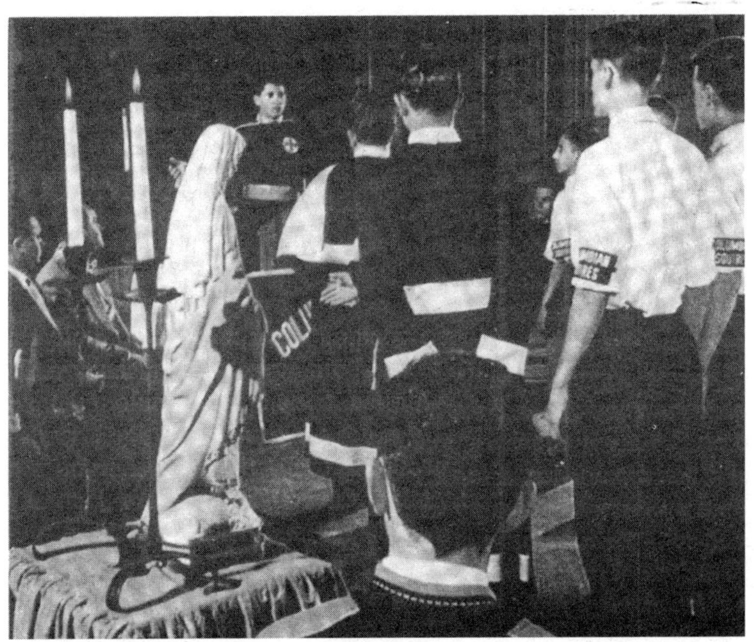

COLUMBIAN SQUIRES (the Knights of Columbus branch for high school boys) in New Haven initiate members. Seated youths already belong. Robed officers explain the importance of their Catholic heritage to the new candidates (in white shirts).

Life Magazine, May 27, 1957

Dr. Rivera said: Oh, yes. In fact, in their oath, you can see how close their alliance is to the pope. They committed themselves to be killed or destroyed if they fail to comply with their oath. They ask the militia of the pope, the Jesuits, to put them to death. They are committed to make America Catholic.

Then I said: Thank God we've had the privilege of printing these books.

And Dr. Rivera said: Yes, the privilege and the blessing of the Lord.

And then I thanked Him.

Life Magazine, May 27, 1957

Let me read something to you: "Life" magazine reviewed one phase of Roman Catholic power in America. The leading story of the May 27th, 1957 edition was devoted to the 75th year of the Knights of Columbus. The pictures, many in full color, depicted the kind of pomp and circumstance which goes into Roman strategy. The legions of Rome are awesome. More than one million practicing Catholics make up the ranks of the Knights of Columbus. They are fraternally pledged to the ideal of bringing America under papal rule. They are powerful, wealthy, loyal. Little wonder that the Pope affectionately describes the Knights as "the right lay arm of the Catholic Church in America."

I believe, if we had kept silent, in 5 years it would have been over. The plans for the take-over would have been in full operation. No one would have been able to withstand it. But because we did go ahead with **ALBERTO,** I believe we knocked back their time-table at least 5 years. And our hope and prayer here is that with the material we're publishing we'll be able to wreck their time-table for at least a generation, that our children can survive before they unleash their holocaust against us.

I can almost hear some of the comments now: "Hey, Chick, that's speculation. You have only Dr. Rivera's word on that. What proof do you have the Vatican wants to destroy or take over the United States?"

Well, most of you have never read the great Christian classic, **50 YEARS IN THE 'CHURCH' OF ROME** by Charles Chiniquy. It was out of print, but we reprinted it at Chick Publications, and believe me, the Jesuits hate this book. I would like to quote the words of Abraham Lincoln regarding the Civil War as found in **50 YEARS IN THE 'CHURCH' OF ROME:** "This war would never have been possible without the sinister influence of the Jesuits. We owe it to popery that we now see our land reddened with the blood of her noblest sons. Though there were great differences of opinion between the South and the North on the question of slavery, neither Jeff Davis nor anyone of the leading men of the Confederacy would have dared to attack the North, had they not relied on the promises of the Jesuits, that, under the mask of Democracy, the money and the arms of the Roman Catholic, even the arms of France were at their disposal, if they would attack us. I pity the priests, the bishops and monks of Rome in the United States, when the people realize that they are, in great part, responsible for the tears and the blood shed in this war. I conceal what I know, on that subject, from the knowledge of the nation; for if the people knew the whole truth, this war would turn into a religious war, and it would at once, take a tenfold more savage and bloody character. It would become merciless as all religious wars are. It would become a war of extermination on both sides. The Protestants of both the North and the South would surely unite to exterminate the priests and the Jesuits, if they could hear what Professor Morse has said to me of the plots made in the very city of Rome to destroy this Republic, and if they could learn how the priests, the nuns, and the monks, which daily land on our shores, under the pretext of preaching their religion, instructing the people in their schools, taking care of the sick in the hospitals, are nothing else but the emissaries of the Pope, of Napoleon, and the other despots of Europe, to undermine our institutions, alienate the hearts of our people from our constitution, and our laws, destroy our schools, and prepare a reign of anarchy here as they have done in Ireland, in Mexico, in Spain, and wherever there are any people who want to be free."

And then President Abraham Lincoln went on to say: "Is it not an absurdity to give to a man a thing which he is sworn to hate, curse, and destroy? And does not the Church of Rome hate, curse and destroy liberty of conscience whenever she can do it safely? I am for liberty of conscience in its noblest, broadest, highest sense. But I cannot give liberty of conscience to the Pope and to his followers, the Papists, so long as they tell me, through all their councils, theologians, and canon laws, that their conscience orders them to bum my wife, strangle my children, and cut my throat when they find their opportunity! This does not seem to be understood by the people today. But sooner or later, the light of common sense will make it clear to every one that no liberty of conscience can be granted to men who are sworn to obey a Pope, who pretends to have the right to put to death those who differ from him in religion."

That, beloved, was said back at the time of the Civil War, and it completely backs up the information Dr. Rivera has given us.

Did you hear that? Were you really listening? Did it sink in what President Abraham Lincoln said? Now think back to that interview I had with Dr. Rivera that I told you about. You've got to understand that when Dr. Rivera was a Jesuit priest under that awful oath and induction, he was in the deepest area of the Vatican's intelligence. He was in the cloak and dagger business for the whore of Revelation. Isn't it logical that the Vatican ***must*** disavow any knowledge of Dr. Rivera's existence? All intelligence agencies do this to their deep agents. It's common knowledge. What you heard on that interview is what Dr. Rivera received in his Vatican briefings given to him by the Jesuit General on how the Roman Catholic Institution plans to take over the United States.

Don't you see that Dr. Rivera is bringing forth the same information, and it completely backs up and coincides with what Abraham Lincoln said, to warn us? And people say that Chick Publications is coming off the wall! While we're sounding the alarm, Rome is pushing as hard as she can in the area of Civil Rights to block our religious freedom and to stop us from calling her the whore of Revelation. Already in Canada, they have banned two of our books, calling them pornography.* They'll move heaven and earth to keep this material out of your hands, and to keep it from being broadcast. I thank God Dr. Rivera arrived on the scene when he did because in a few short years we would have all been muzzled.

Is what I'm saying sinking in? Beloved, now when you turn on the evening news, you'll see it in a different light because you're going to see the hand of Rome in world politics.

Let's wake up, beloved. We're not a bunch of little two-year-olds anymore. Pastors need to wake up. You deacons and church members need to wake up because your kids are going to be destroyed in a few short years if you don't. I'm referring especially to those pastors who are pushing bubbly love

*Just before going to press, word was received that the Canadian Protestant League had successfully challenged the Canadian government in court and the ban had been lifted.

to everyone, and who turn white and break into a cold sweat when anything controversial comes along. Do you think the priests of Rome respect you for that? Let me tell you, pastors, they hate the ground you walk on and hold you in nothing but contempt. They secretly look at you like scum under their feet. I was recently told that in 1949, an ex-Jesuit priest told a Rev. Eubanks in California, that when the Vatican takes control of the United States, every pastor and his family will be shot in the head.

You know, we sent a copy of **THE GODFATHERS** to 100 local pastors, and do you know how many had the courage, or the courtesy, to respond? Not one. You know the Bible says that judgment begins in the house of God. And unless we wake up, it's going to happen here.

If the pastors are men, then let's act like men of God and start thundering the Word of God from the pulpits. The thin line is in the pulpits holding back the forces of hell. Once that caves in, it will be underground churches for America. And then they're going to hunt us down like rats, And they'll show us as much mercy as they did in Yugoslavia. Remember, the priest said it was not a sin to kill a child of 7. Only this time, there will be no United States to defend you. Where are you going to run? To Mexico? It's gone. Canada? It's almost gone. Ireland? Forget it. They're picking it off now. No place to go, beloved. Only to the Lord, and time is running out. We are on a razor's edge. It's time to get on our knees and stop this fooling around, and putting on the pious act.

If your pastor doesn't have the courage to stand against Rome, you need to make him aware of this information, and that it is his responsibility to make his people aware of it too. And if he won't, then you must make the stand.

You can now expect to see the supporters of the Vatican start blasting Chiniquy for daring to quote Abraham Lincoln in his book, **50 YEARS IN THE 'CHURCH' OF ROME.** We're in a war, beloved, and I thank God the Lord has directed us to prepare the ammunition you'll need from Chick Publications to give you back-up and background, and you'll know how to face the lost

John Paul II, "Pilgrimage of Faith"

Pope John Paul II in Washington D.C.

Roman Catholics after you've gone into prayer. Because, if you don't turn into a soulwinning church, the whore is going to have you and your grandchildren for breakfast. Have you already forgotten the screams that filled the night air in Paris during the St. Bartholomew massacre? Have you forgotten the little pregnant mothers tied to the tree branches, begging for mercy in Ireland while the dogs were fighting underneath for their unborn children? And the bloody knives in the hands of those smirking fanatics driven on by their priests to butcher these Christian ladies? Have you forgotten these bloodbaths that were quoted in Foxe's Book of Martyrs? The Vatican wants you to forget it. Have you forgotten what took place in Yugoslavia ... Catholic priests impaling children on stakes as they screamed in agony in 1940? You better ***never*** forget it! And don't forget that it was at a time of peace, love and kindness just before each attack, just like today, beloved. And don't you forget one million Knights of Columbus in the United States have sworn to turn America into a papal state. God help us. You don't think it's coming here? You don't think history repeats itself? It's time to get sober and turn into spiritual soldiers, and start arming yourselves with the helmet of salvation and the shield of faith, and the sword of the Spirit, realizing the forces of darkness ***can*** be held back.

We have a common enemy, beloved. It's time to get back to Christ, and start showing mercy and compassion to the precious Roman Catholic people who have been betrayed by their leaders. If we don't, their blood will be on our hands. We must make an effort to win them to Christ.

CONCLUSION

Does this mean our fight is with the Roman Catholic people who have been betrayed by their leaders? No. Our battle is with the whore of Revelation, the mother of harlots and abominations of the earth. God tells us to attack this system. And our job is to rip that mask off her face, and let those poor Roman Catholics see what they're really tied to - the bondage, the fact that they're all going into the lake of fire. They have to be set free. They have to find Christ as the answer. It's not Mary and the rest of the unscriptural garbage they throw on them. It's our job to try to win them to Christ.

Beloved, we're not out to please pastors, or churches, or denominations. We are out to please Christ. We've laid everything on the line. It's His war. It's His battle. He's blessed us. We're doubling the size of our facilities, in faith, because I know God is raising an army, and we're going to win these precious Roman Catholics. And that's what it's all about. WIN these people! Don't throw rocks at them! We're not Nazi's. We're not Ku Klux Klanners. We care about these people. But it's not the selfish, worldly love being taught so much today, that would rather watch them go to hell, than to risk offending them with the truth. We've put everything on the line to try to win them to Christ. And by God's grace, we will. Catholics are being saved all over this country. In fact, it's getting so big, that those in the Vatican are getting worried. Praise God, we now see the light in the tunnel. Catholics ***are*** being saved. We hear the rumblings across the country where people are opening their eyes and blinking and saying, "Good night, what Chick is saying is true." And they're beginning to read some of these books like

THE SECRET HISTORY OF THE JESUITS, and **50 YEARS IN THE 'CHURCH' OF ROME.** We're seeing priests and nuns coming to Christ and leaving the Roman system. We've seen the phonies come up, but we've seen the real ones coming out now. There's an upheaval coming, beloved, and it's going to gain momentum. It's time now we got on our knees to be broken before Christ and cry to the Lord that these Roman Catholics get saved, because it's the power of God that's going to move through us. The fields are white unto harvest, and ***now*** is the hour to pick up the gospel and go forward and ***win*** these precious souls to Christ.

God bless you, and thank you for taking the time to read this book.

P. S.

Remember back when the John Birch Societies were springing up all over the United States, with people screaming "This is it! The communists are coming!" "They're taking us over. We've only got a few years left." Remember that? ... The excitement and the fervor of Christians rallying to fight this monster, even if it meant joining forces with the Roman Catholics, to stop it? Beloved, it was a great smokescreen to take the eyes of the Christians off the movements of the Vatican and her push for world control.

Lo, and behold! Here it comes again. Only the names have been changed. The newest movement has been called the "New Age Movement," and it's in full force. But who's behind it?

We know this is an abomination, and the Bible tells us that the mother of abominations is the whore of Revelation 17, the Roman Catholic institution. Rest assured, the Jesuits, the Illuminati, the Opus Dei, and Masons are guiding its activities, and the result will be another gigantic smokescreen which is already taking the eyes of the Christians off the Vatican while they secretly use this movement to accomplish their goals.

Bishop Fulton Sheen attacked communism in the past, and although it is a by-product, they will viciously attack it to accomplish their goals. Catholics will try to rally the Christians together to attack "The New Age Movement." The Christians are already steamed up on this, and the Jesuits are laughing their heads off.

Dear Jack,

I grew up in West Germany in a mostly catholic area and learned some of those things you said. I personally remember seeing the steel cages hanging from the steeples of the cathedral in Munster in which Ana-Baptists were starved to death until the birds ate their flesh, These cages could be seen 27 years ago. I don't know if they are still there. I personally believe that the half has not been told.

W. K., Linden, N.J.